2∞

A STUDENT BOOK

Amazing English!™

AN INTEGRATED ESL CURRICULUM

Addison-Wesley Publishing Company

Copyright © 1996 by Addison-Wesley Publishing Company, Inc. This work is based in part on *Addison-Wesley ESL*, copyright © 1992, 1989 by Addison-Wesley Publishing Company, Inc. All rights reserved. No part of this publication may be reproduced, stored in a retrieval system, or transmitted in any form or by any means, electronic, mechanical, photocopying, recording, or otherwise without the prior written permission of the publisher. Printed in the United States of America.

ISBN 0-201-85343-4 Softbound
4 5 6 7 8 9 10-BAM-00 99 98 97

ISBN 0-201-49143-5 Hardbound
2 3 4 5 6 7 8 9 10-BAM-00 99 98 97

CONTENTS

Theme 1 School Days — 3

What Can We Do...? (song)	3
Let's Build a Playground! (photo essay)	4
The Alphabet Cheer! (song/chant) Bob Schneider	7
What Are Kids Like? (excerpt from Kids) Catherine and Laurence Anholt	8
I Spy...School Supplies (photo puzzle)	10
Another Week of School: Holistic Assessment Story	12
Spin and Draw: Holistic Assessment Game	13
Hands-On Math: "What Color is Your Hair?"	14

Theme 2 At Home — 15

Mom (poem) Tanaka Datsuke	15
In My Mother's House (excerpt) Ann Nolan Clark	16
Goodnight, Juma (poem) Eloise Greenfield	19
Tortillas (Latino rhyme)	22
What Are You Wearing Today? (song) Bob Schneider	23
Baby Bear's Lunch: Holistic Assessment Story	24
A Walk Through the Woods: Holistic Assessment Game	25
Hands-On Social Studies: "Family Trees"	26

Theme 3 More About Me — 27

Sometimes (poem) Mary Ann Hoberman	27
Terrible, Terrible Tiger (poem) Colin and Jacqui Hawkins	28
Today, Today, Today! (song) Bob Schneider	32
Look Closely (photo puzzle)	33
If You're Happy and You Know It (song)	35
Best Friends: Holistic Assessment Story	36
Guess Who?: Holistic Assessment Game	37
Hands-On Math: "Shape People"	38

Theme 4 Everybody Eats — 39

Spaghetti (chant)	39
Shopping (excerpt from Words and Pictures) Siobhan Dodds	40
I Like Pizza (jump rope rhyme)	42
Two Greedy Bears (Eastern European folktale)	44
Peanut Butter and Jelly Song (song)	49
The Woman and the Gingerbread Man: Holistic Assessment Story	50
Shopping Cart Race: Holistic Assessment Game	51
Hands-On Math: "Salsa Recipe"	52

Theme 5 Farm and Forest — 53

The Farm is in a Flurry (poem) Jack Prelutsky	53
Cock-A-Doodle-Doo! (excerpt) Marc Robinson	54
Down on Grandpa's Farm (song)	58
Three Little Monkeys (rhyme)	59
Baby Barn Owls (photo essay)	60
Wedding Day: Holistic Assessment Story	62
Are You Ready?: Holistic Assessment Game	63
Hands-On Science: "How Do They Move?"	64

Theme 6 Outside My Window — 65

I'm Glad the Sky is Painted Blue (poem)	65
I Spy...A Butterfly (photo puzzle)	66
See for Yourself (Asian folktale)	68
City Gardens (photo essay)	72
The Wheels on the Bus (song)	75
The Most Wonderful Dinner: Holistic Assessment Story	76
How's the Weather: Holistic Assessment Game	77
White Sheep, White Sheep (poem)	78
Hands-On Science: "Make a Sundial"	79
Index	80

School Days

THEME 1

What can we do when we all go out,
All go out, all go out?
What can we do when we all go out,
When we all go out to play?

Let's Build A Playground!

We want a playground.
We talk and draw pictures.
The grown-ups listen.

Art | Math | Music
Science | Social Studies
LANGUAGE ARTS

Theme 1

It's building day!

We all work together.

School Days 5

Look! It's all done!
We love our playground.

The Alphabet Cheer!

Give me an A! — A!
Give me a B! — B!
Give me an ABCDEFG! — ABCDEFG!
Give me an H! — H!
Give me an I! — I!
Give me an HIJKLMNOP! — HIJKLMNOP!
Give me a Q! — Q!
Give me an R! — R!
Give me a QRSTUVW! — QRSTUVW!
Give me an X! — X!
Give me a Y! — Y!
Give me a Z! — Z!
So tell me now,
What did you get? — I think we got
The alphabet!

WHAT ARE KIDS LIKE?

EXCERPTED FROM *KIDS*
BY CATHERINE AND LAURENCE ANHOLT

Kids are silly, kids are funny.

Kids have noses that are runny.

Some kids wash but some are muddy,

Both kinds have a favorite buddy.

I Spy
... School Supplies

I spy a rabbit,
   eleven bears in all,
A dog on a block,
   a seal on a ball;

One red bottle,
   one rubber band,
A popsicle stick, and
   the letters in HAND.

School Days

11

LISTEN   **S**PEAK

Another Week of School

1.
2.
3.
4.
5. My Family

12   Theme 1

READ **WRITE** **THINK!**

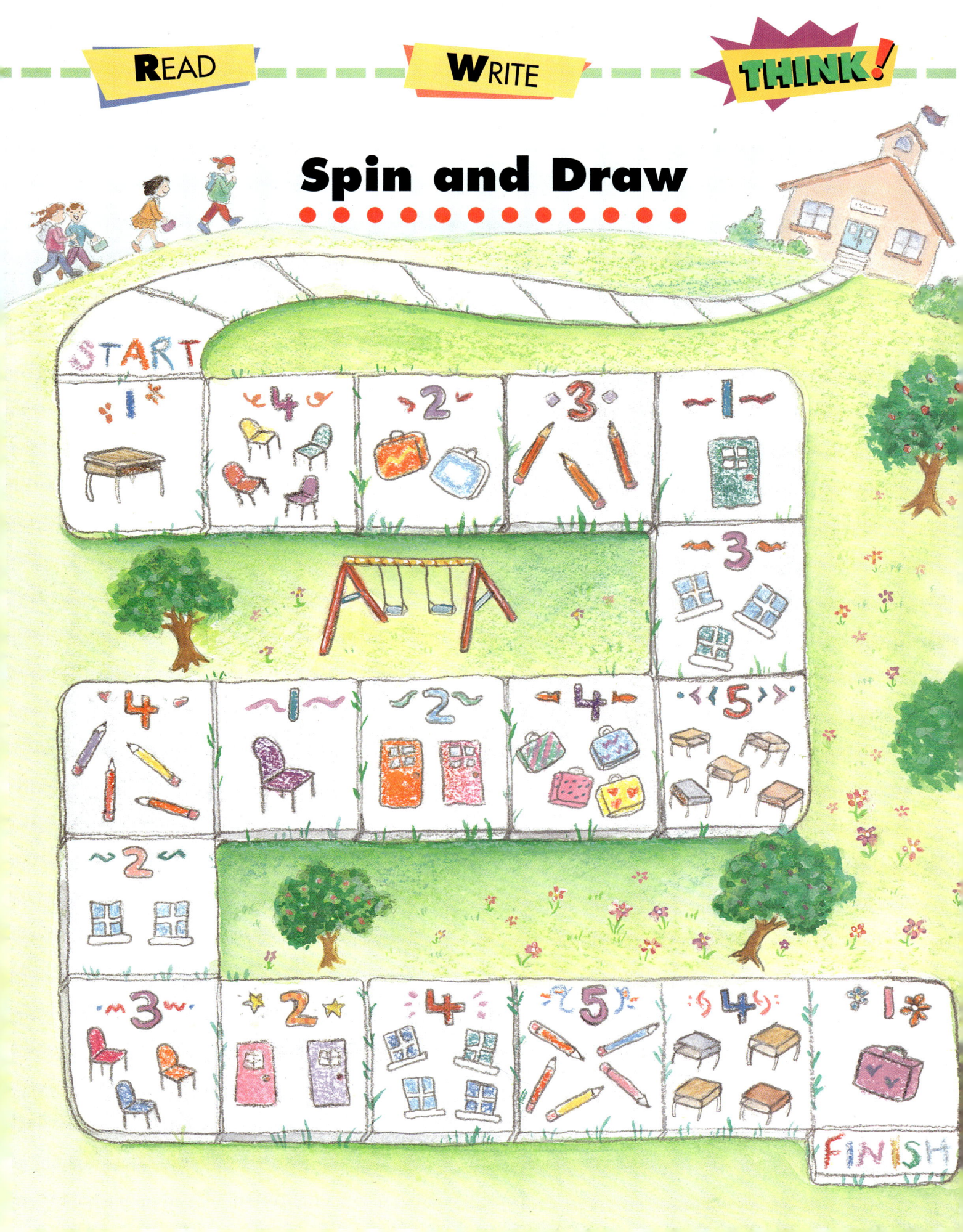

Spin and Draw

Hands-On Math

What color is your hair?

Red
- Donny
- Bill

Black
- Jesse
- Anna
- Louis

Brown
- Lisa
- Linda
- Maria

Blonde
- Lilly
- Jake
- Susan

Theme 1

At Home

THEME 2

MOM

Hey mom–
Do you know why I was born?
I wanted to meet you, mom,
so I got born.

Tanaka Datsuke, age 6

IN MY MOTHER'S HOUSE

EXCERPTED FROM THE BOOK
BY ANN NOLAN CLARK

In my Mother's house
All day
I play and work;
All night
I sleep .

The walls come
　　close around me
In a good way.

I can see them;
I can feel them;
I live with them.

At Home

This house is good to me,
It keeps me;
I like it,
My Mother's house.

Goodnight, Juma

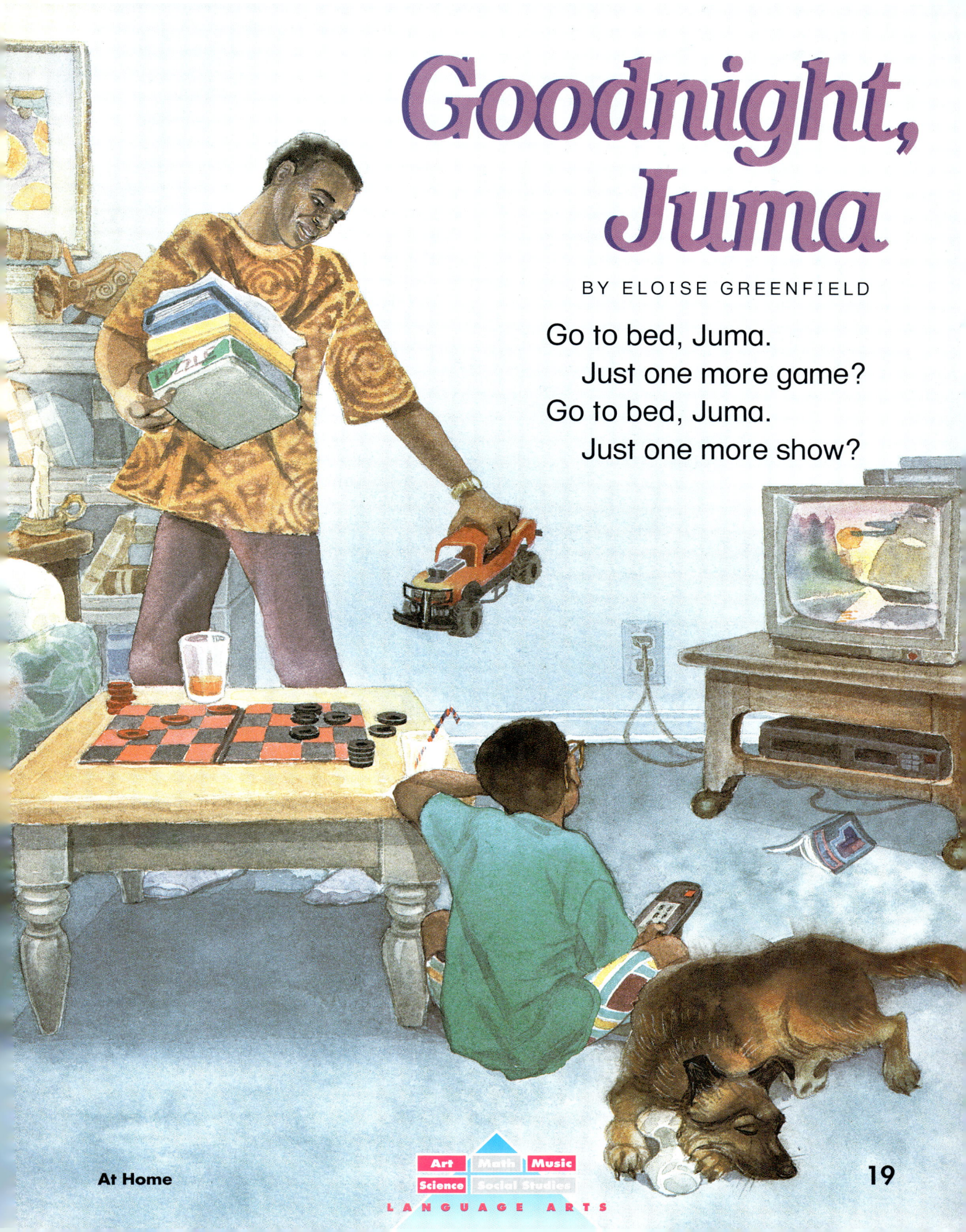

BY ELOISE GREENFIELD

Go to bed, Juma.
    Just one more game?
Go to bed, Juma.
    Just one more show?

At Home

19

Go to bed, Juma.
   Just one more minute?
Juma, go to bed,
I said.

Just —
No.
—a hug?
Oh. You bet.

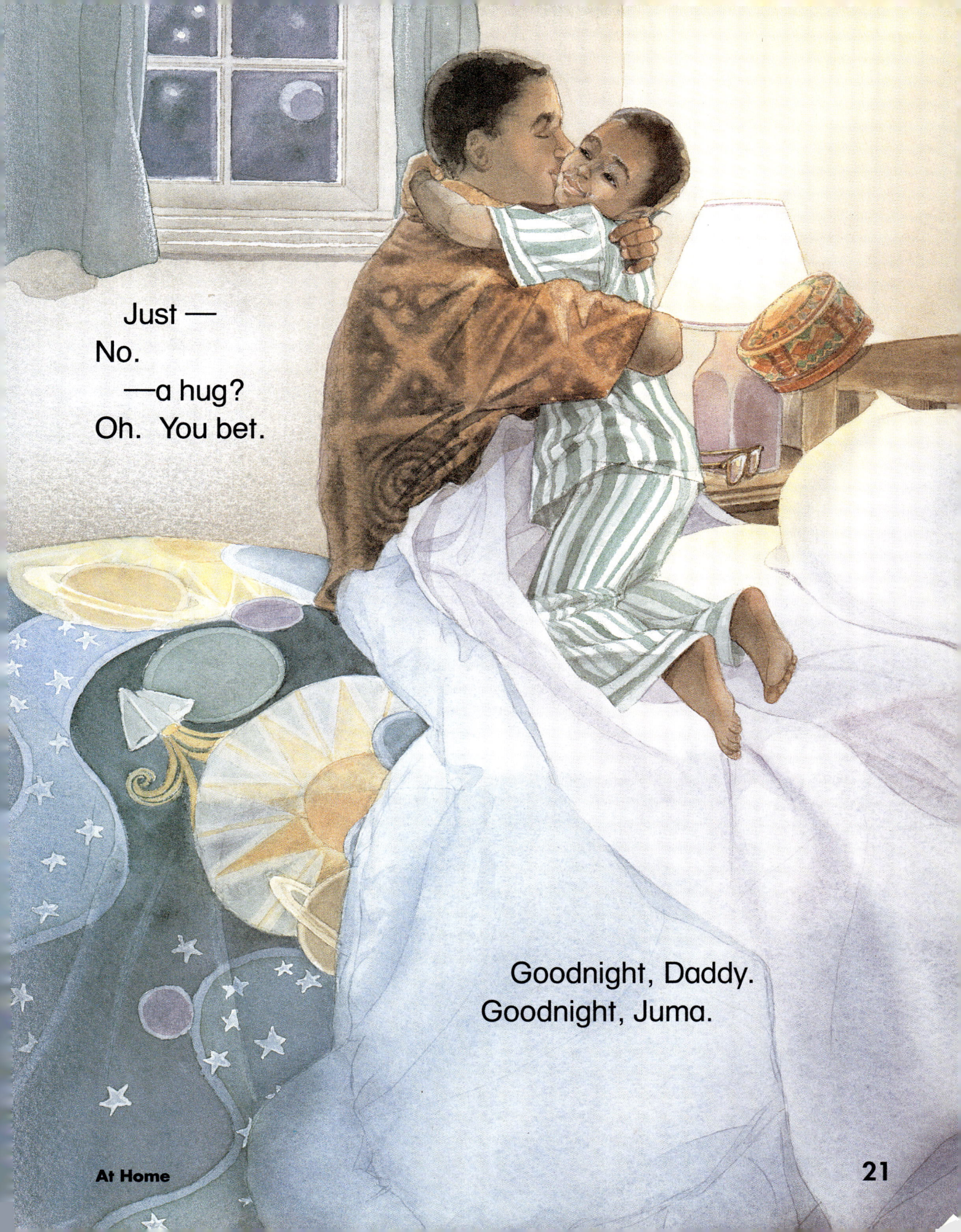

Goodnight, Daddy.
Goodnight, Juma.

Tortillas

Tortillas, tortillas
Tortillas para mamá.
Tortillas, tortillas
Tortillas para papá.
Tortillas, tortillas
Tortillas para mí!

Tortillas, tortillas
Tortillas for my mother.
Tortillas, tortillas
Tortillas for my father.
Tortillas, tortillas
Tortillas for me!

What Are You Wearing Today?

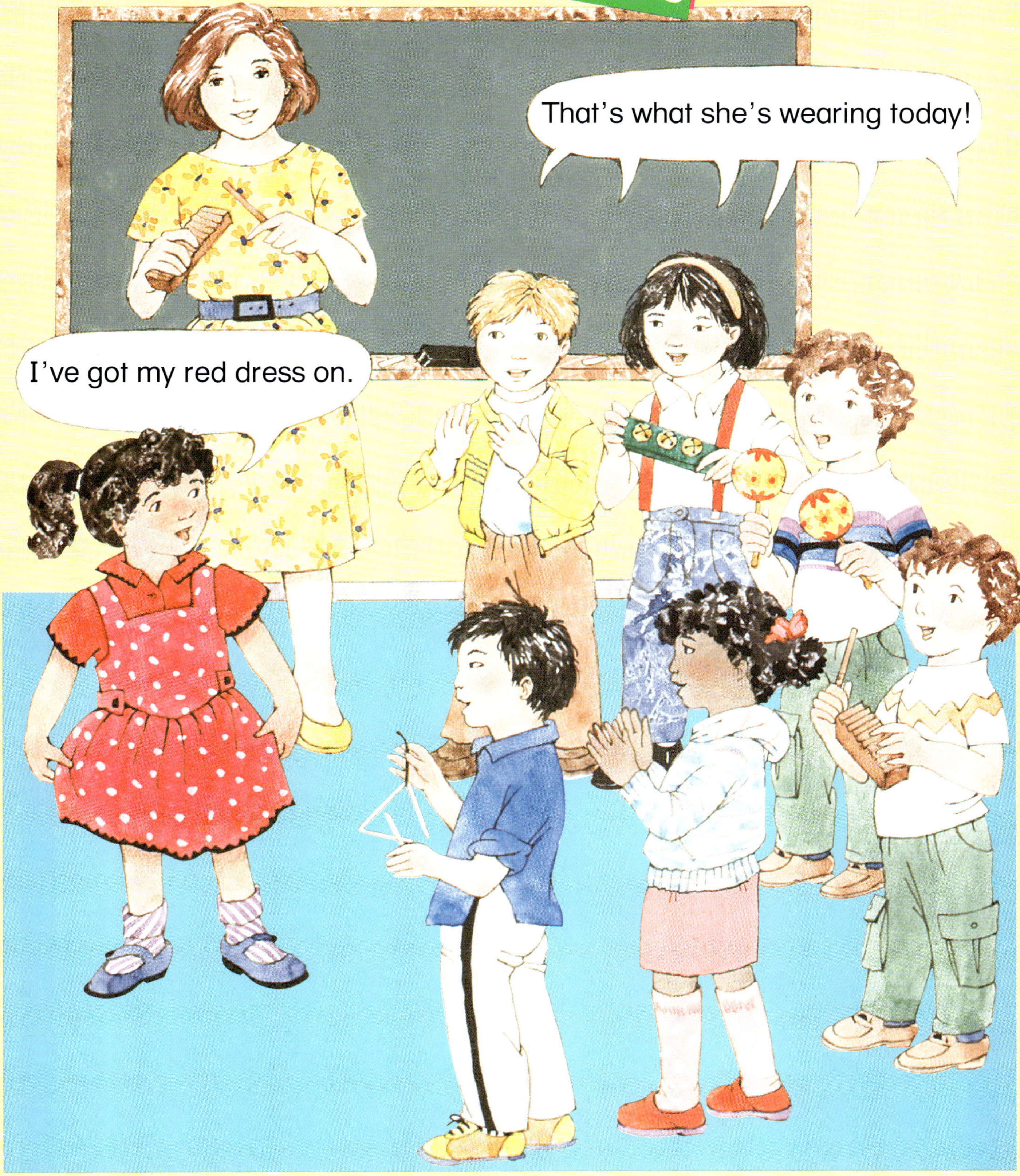

LISTEN **SPEAK**

Baby Bear's Lunch

A Walk Through the Woods

Hands-On Social Studies

Family Trees

Theme 2

More About Me

THEME 3

SOMETIMES

Sometimes I like to be alone
And look up at the sky
And think my thoughts inside my head—
Just me, myself, and I.

Mary Ann Hoberman

27

Terrible, Terrible Tiger

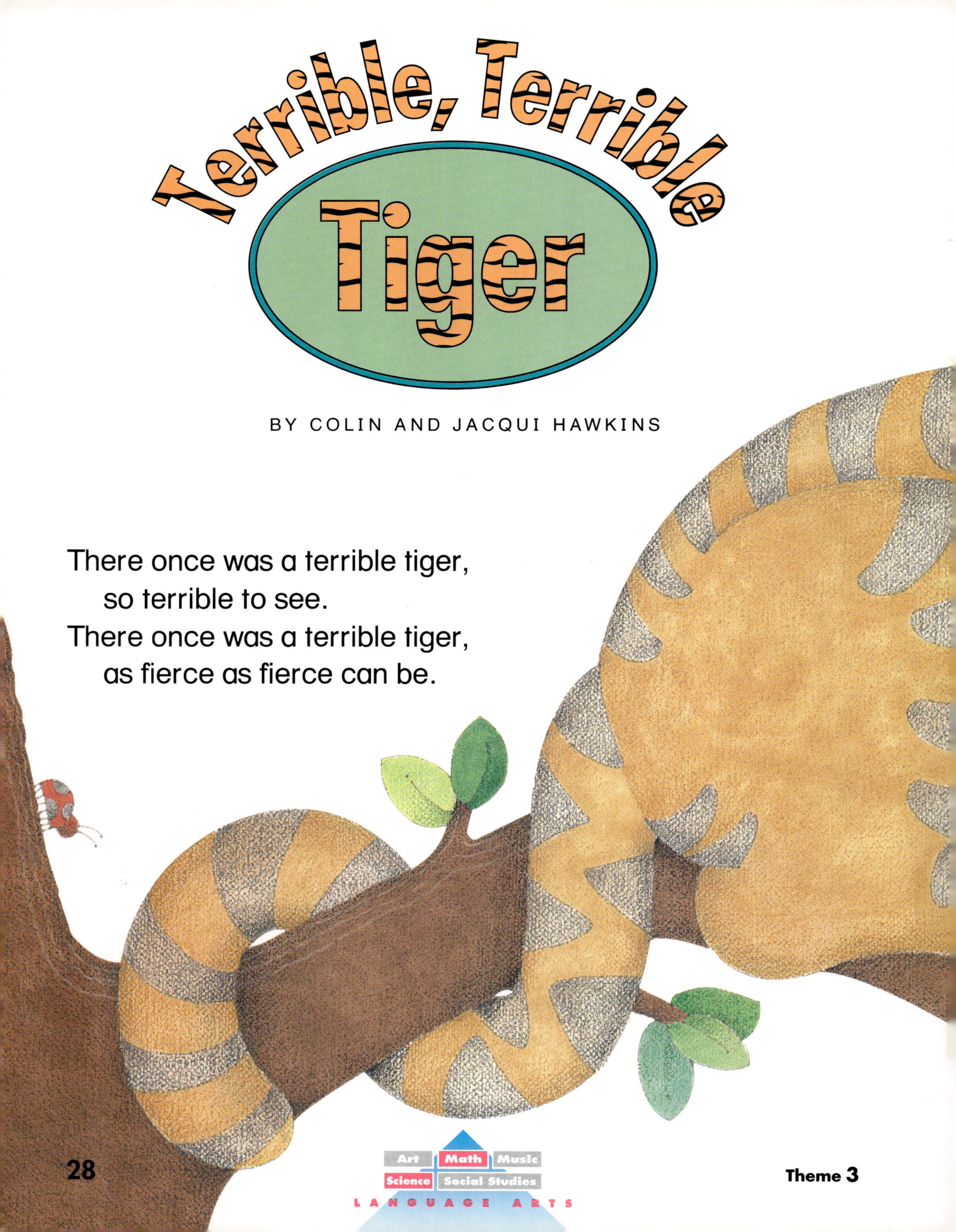

BY COLIN AND JACQUI HAWKINS

There once was a terrible tiger,
   so terrible to see.
There once was a terrible tiger,
   as fierce as fierce can be.

There once was a terrible tiger
 that looked down from a tree.
There once was a terrible tiger
 that came creeping after me.

There once was a terrible tiger
   with teeth as sharp as sharp could be.
That terrible, terrible tiger —
   will he eat ME?
That terrible, terrible tiger,
   he roared … and leapt at me.

I cuddled that terrible tiger.
He's really my kitten, you see.

Today, Today, Today

What are you going to do today?

She's going to ride her bike today.
Today, today, today, today.

I'm going to ride my bike today!

Theme 3

Look Closely

All these things belong to me. Look carefully. What do you see?

Open your mouth!

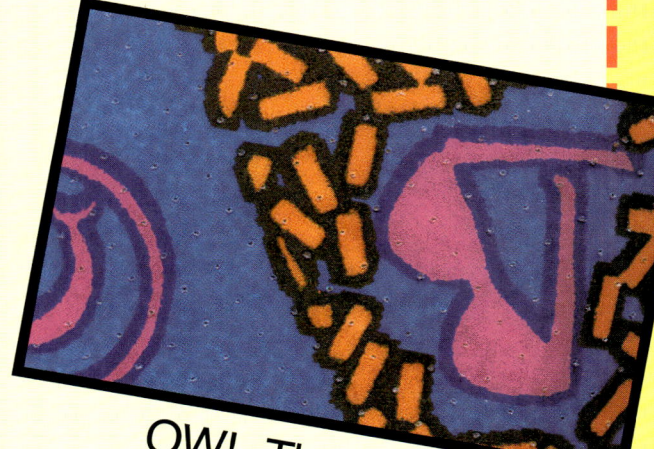

OW! That hurts.

What are these?

Turn the page

More About Me

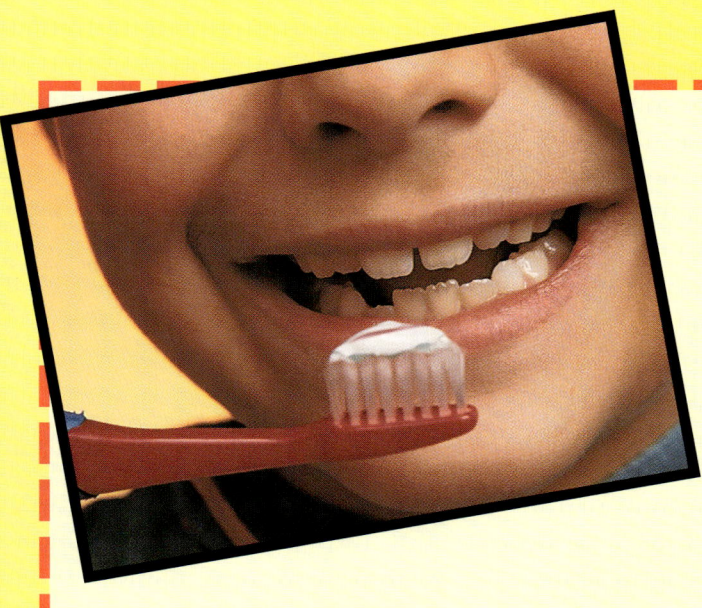

It's a toothbrush.

It's a band-aid.

They're crayons.

If You're Happy and You Know It

1. Hee! Hee! Hee!
2. Grrrrr!!
3. WAAH!!
4. Eeek!
5. Mmmm!!
6. Zzzz!

More About Me

LISTEN　　　　　　**SPEAK**

Best Friends

1

2

3

4

36　　　　　　　　　　　　　　　　　Theme 3

READ   **W**RITE   **T**HINK!

Guess Who?

Hands-On Math

Everybody Eats

THEME 4

Spaghetti on my plate,
Spaghetti on my plate,
Twirl it up, twirl it up,
Spaghetti on my plate.

Shopping

EXCERPTED FROM *WORDS AND PICTURES*
BY SIOBHAN DODDS

Mommy puts the  potatoes,

carrots, and  bananas

in her  basket.

I carry the  peas,

mushrooms, and  apples

in mine.

Everybody Eats

I Like Pizza

I like pizza.
You like pie.
We like jumping
Very high.

I like tacos.
You like toast.
Of all my friends,
I like you most.

Everybody Eats

Two Greedy Bears

A FOLKTALE FROM EASTERN EUROPE

Once there were two little bears named Magda and Josef. They were friends, but they argued a lot.

One day Magda and Josef saw something by the side of the road.

What is it?

I don't know. Let's see.

It's cheese!

A big, round cheese!

The two greedy little bears began to argue.

"I saw it first. It's mine."

"Give it to me!"

"I know. Let's share it."

"No, I saw it first. It's mine."

"No, give it to me!"

Everybody Eats

So, Josef cut the cheese into two pieces.
But Magda was not happy.

"You have more than me."

"Yes, you do."

"No, I don't."

"No, I don't."

A fox came out of the woods.

"Why are you arguing?"

"Josef has more cheese than me."

"OK. I'll take a little bite from Josef's cheese."

"Now Magda has more than me!"

"OK. I'll take a little bite from Magda's cheese."

Everybody Eats

The fox kept taking little bites, first from Josef's cheese, and then from Magda's cheese. Finally, he stopped.

Look! Now it's perfect! Your pieces are exactly the same size.

Yes, but they're tiny!

You ate almost the whole cheese!

Yes, I know. And it was delicious. Next time, don't argue so much. And don't be so greedy!

Peanut Butter and Jelly Song

1
2
3
4
5
6

Everybody Eats

49

LISTEN **SPEAK**

The Woman and the Gingerbread Man

1 I'm hungry.

2

3

4

READ   **W**RITE   **THINK**!

Shopping Cart Race

HANDS-ON MATH

SALSA RECIPE

1 can whole tomatoes

1/4 cup chopped onions

1/2 teaspoon vinegar

1 tablespoon oil

1 teaspoon oregano

1 teaspoon chopped parsley

1. Crush the tomatoes. Put them in a bowl.
2. Add the rest of the ingredients.
3. Stir well.

Farm and Forest

THEME 5

The farm is in a flurry,
The rooster's caught the flu—
His cock-a-doodle-doo has changed
To cock-a-doodle-chooooooo!

Jack Prelutsky

53

Cock-A-Doodle-Doo
What Does It Sound Like to You?

EXCERPTED FROM THE BOOK BY MARC ROBINSON

Does a rooster always crow
COCK-A-DOODLE-DOO?
To me it does—and
maybe to you, too.

From *Cock-A-Doodle-Doo! What Does It Sound Like to You?* copyright © 1993 Marc Robinson and Steve Jenkins. Reprinted by permission of Stewart, Tabori & Chang, Inc.

CoCK-A-DOoDLE-DoO!

Farm and Forest

But to Spaniards, roosters cry KEE-KEE-REE-KEE!
Now how, can you tell me, just how can that be?

KEE-KEE-REE-KEE!

And to the Japanese, did you know, a rooster calls KOH-KEH-KOH-KOH!

KOH-KEH-KOH-KOH!

Farm and Forest

Down on Grandpa's Farm

58   Theme 5

Three Little Monkeys

1

2

3

Farm and Forest

BABY BARN OWLS

Baby owls hatch out of eggs.
The babies are covered with soft, fluffy feathers.

Owl parents cuddle their babies to keep them warm.

Barn owls are very good hunters.
They hunt at night.
They catch mice for their hungry babies!

LISTEN　　　SPEAK

Wedding Day

1
2
3
4

READ **WRITE** **THINK!**

Are You Ready?

Hands-On Science

How Do They Move?

| hop | swim | walk | fly | wiggle |

64   Art · Math · Music · Science · Social Studies · LANGUAGE ARTS   Theme 5

Outside My Window

THEME 6

I'm glad the sky is painted blue,
And the earth is painted green,
With such a lot of nice fresh air
All sandwiched in between.

I Spy
... A Butterfly

I spy an arrowhead,
   a little white goose,
A horse's shadow,
   a snake on the loose;

One egg that's white,
   another that's blue,
A tiger in the grass,
   and a small turtle, too.

Outside My Window

SEE FOR YOURSELF

A FOLKTALE FROM ASIA

CHARACTERS:

Storyteller | Rabbit | Fox | Monkey | Elephant | Lion

Storyteller: A long time ago a rabbit lived by a lake. One day a piece of fruit fell from a tree. It landed in the lake.
KERPLUNK!

Rabbit was scared.

Rabbit: I must go and tell Fox.

Run, run, run for your life.
KERPLUNK is coming after us!

Storyteller Fox ran along with Rabbit.

Fox We must go and tell Monkey.

Run, run, run for your life.
KERPLUNK is coming after us!

Storyteller Monkey ran along with Fox and Rabbit.

Monkey We must go and tell Elephant.

Run, run, run for your life.
KERPLUNK is coming after us!

Storyteller: Elephant, Monkey, Fox, and Rabbit ran through the forest.

Lion: Stop!
What is all the noise about?
Why are you running away?

Elephant: Run, run, run for your life!
KERPLUNK is coming after us.

Lion: How do you know?

Elephant: Monkey told me.

Monkey: Fox told me.

Fox: Rabbit told me.

Storyteller: Just then another piece of fruit fell into the lake. KERPLUNK!

Rabbit: It's the big KERPLUNK. Run, run!

Lion: Ha, ha, ha! You silly, silly animals!

Fox: Wait! That was just a piece of fruit falling from a tree. There is no big KERPLUNK!

Lion: That's right, Fox. No KERPLUNK! Next time, don't believe everything Rabbit says. Go see for yourself!

Outside My Window

City Gardens

In many cities, people are building gardens. Grown-ups and children clean up the land. They bring new soil to the garden.

In the spring, the people plant seeds. Soon little plants come up.

The people water the plants and pull the weeds. The plants grow bigger and bigger.

In the summer, people meet in the garden.
They smell the sweet flowers.
They pick fresh vegetables to eat for dinner.
The gardens are lovely green places in the middle of the city.

The Wheels on the Bus

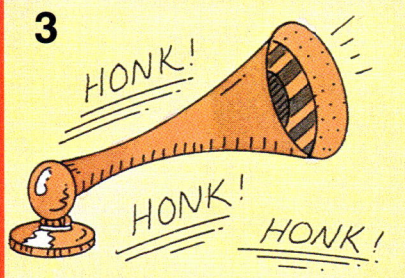

Outside My Window

75

LISTEN   **SPEAK**

The Most Wonderful Dinner

1
2
3
4
5

76   Theme 6

READ **W**RITE **THINK!**

How's the Weather?

START

FINISH

White Sheep, White Sheep

White sheep, white sheep
  on a blue hill,
When the wind stops
  you all stand still.

You all run away
  when the wind blows.
White sheep, white sheep,
  where do you go?

Hands-On Science

Clocks and watches show time.

A sundial is a clock.

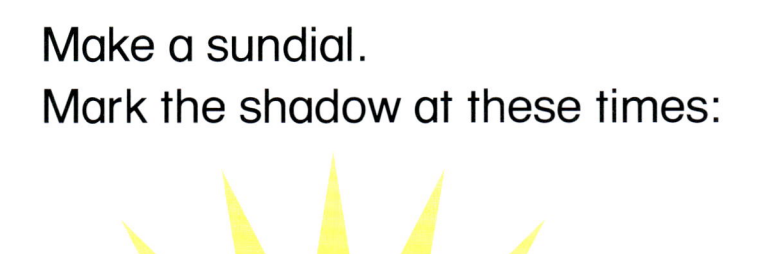

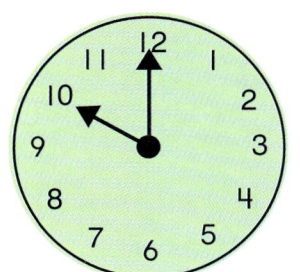

• •

Make a sundial.
Mark the shadow at these times:

ten o'clock

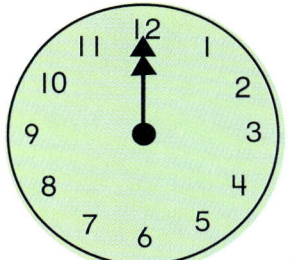

twelve o'clock

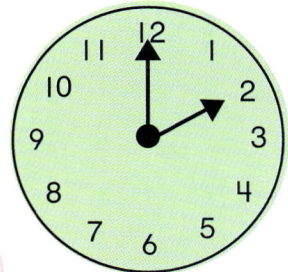

two o'clock

Outside My Window

INDEX

TYPES OF LITERATURE
Contemporary fiction 8–9, 16–18, 28–31, 40–41, 54–57
Multicultural folktales 44–48, 68–71
Photo essays 4–6, 33–34, 60–61, 72–74
Poetry 8–9, 10–11, 15, 16–18, 19–21, 27, 28–31, 39, 53, 65, 66, 78
Songs, rhymes, and chants 3, 7, 22, 23, 32, 35, 42–43, 49, 58, 59, 75

TOPICS
Alphabet 7
Animals 10–11, 28–31, 53, 54–57, 58, 59, 60–61, 64, 66–67, 68–71
Art 12, 14
Body parts 14, 38
City life 72–74, 75
Clothing 23
Colors 10–11, 14, 23, 65, 66
Diversity 8–9, 14, 54–57
Families 15, 16–18, 19–21, 22, 26, 60–61
Feelings 15, 27, 35, 65
Food 22, 39, 40–41, 42–43, 44–48, 49, 52
Friends 4–6, 8–9, 24–25, 36–37, 42–43, 44–48
Gardens 72–74
Home/household routines 16–18, 19–21
Math 14, 38, 44–48, 52
Music 3, 23, 32, 35, 49, 75
Nature and weather 65, 66, 72–74, 78
Personal characteristics 14
Personal preferences 27, 42–43
Pets 28–31
Playgrounds 3, 4–6
School/school routines 3, 4–6, 7, 10–11, 12–13
Science 33–34, 60–61, 64, 66, 72–74, 79
Seasons 72–74
Sequencing 49
Shapes 38
Sharing, working together 4–6, 44–48, 72–74
Shopping 40–41
Social studies 4–6, 16–18, 22, 26, 72–74
Time 79

ACTIVITIES
Classifying 64
Counting 59
Creating new verses to songs and poems 23, 32, 35, 39, 42–43
Enjoying a humorous selection 8–9, 28–31, 53, 59, 68–71
Following directions 13, 25, 37, 51, 63, 77
Graphing 14
Learning about
    building a playground 4–6
    diverse cultures 16–18, 22, 52, 54–57
    food shopping 40
    animal sounds in different languages 54–57
    baby barn owls 60–61
    planting a garden 72–74
Listening to/discussing a story 12, 24, 36, 50, 62, 76
Listening to/reading
    a photo essay 4–6, 60–61, 72–74
    a play 68–71
    a story 44–48, 54–57
Listening to/reciting
    a poem 7, 8–9, 10, 15, 16–18, 19–21, 22, 27, 28–31, 53, 65, 66, 78
    a rhyme or chant 7, 22, 39, 42–43, 49, 59
Listening to/singing a song 3, 23, 32, 35, 49, 58, 75
Playing a board game 13, 25, 37, 51, 63, 77
Predicting 33
Projects
    making a family tree 26
    making a hair color graph 14
    making a sundial 79
    making an animal-classification chart 64
    making salsa 52
    making shape people 38
Reciting the alphabet 7
Solving photo riddles and puzzles 10–11, 33–34, 66–67

LINGUISTIC SKILLS
a/an 7
Commands 7, 19–21, 35, 44–48, 52
Descriptive adjectives 10–11, 23, 58, 66–67, 78
Future tense verbs (going to) 32
Modals
    can 3, 16–18
    must 68–71
Past tense verbs 28–31, 44–48, 68–71
Possessives 22, 23, 27
Prepositions
    around 16–18
    for 22
    in 16–18
    on 10–11, 39
Present progressive tense verbs 23
Present tense verbs 4–6, 8–9, 16–18, 40–41, 42–43, 44–48, 60–61, 64, 72–74
Singular/plural nouns 10–11, 33–34, 40–41, 66–67

HOLISTIC ASSESSMENT
Listening/speaking/thinking skills 12, 24, 36, 50, 62, 76
Playing a game/recognizing print 13, 25, 37, 51, 63, 77

A Publication of the World Language Division

Director of Product Development: Judith M. Bittinger
Executive Editor: Elinor Chamas
Content Development: Elly Schottman, Susan Hooper
Editorial Development: Elly Schottman
Text and Cover Design: Taurins Design Associates
Art Direction and Production: Taurins Design Associates
Production and Manufacturing: James W. Gibbons

Illustrators: Teresa Anderko 75, 79; Ellen Appleby 7; Greta Buchart 53; Yvonne Cathcart 12–13; Chi Chung 52; Maryann Cocca 3, 39; Diane Harris 65; Joy Keenan 19–21; Karen Loccisano 36–37; Paul Moschell 78; Sharron O'Neil 59; Diane Paterson 32; John Sandford 49, 50–51; Yuri Salzman 76–77; Karen Schmidt 24–25, 68–71; Jerry Smath 58; Gilles Tibo 44–48; Rosario Valderrama 27; Fabricio Vanden Broeck 62–63; Marsha Winborn 23, 35; Julie Young 28–31.

Photographers: Ron Austing, Photo Researchers top 61; Phil A. Dotson, Photo Researchers bottom 61; D. Gonzalez bottom left 73, left 74; Richard Hutchings 26, 42–43, 52, 64; Marcia Keegan 16–18; Ken Lax 14; George Mastellone 6, 33–34; Tom McCarthy, Rainbow 15; Leonard Lee Rue III, Photo Researchers 60; Rutgers Urban Gardening top 73, right 74; Joseph Schyler, Stock Boston 72; Peter Tenzer, 38, 79.

Acknowledgements: Pages 4–5, photographs courtesy of Leathers & Associates, Inc. Pages 8–9, "What Are Kids Like?" from *Kids* © 1992 Catherine and Laurence Anholt. Published in the UK by Walker Books Limited. Pages 10–11, "I Spy School Supplies" from *I Spy: A Book of Picture Riddles* by Jean Marzollo and Walter Wick. Text copyright © 1992 by Jean Marzollo; illustrations and photography copyright © 1992 by Walter Wick. Reprinted by permission of Scholastic Inc. Page 15, "Mom" from *Festival In My Heart* by Bruno Navasky, published by Harry N. Abrams, Inc., New York. Pages 16–18, "Home, Home" from *In My Mother's House* by Ann Nolan Clark. Copyright © 1941 by Ann Nolan Clark, renewed © 1969 by Ann Nolan Clark. Used by permission of Viking Penguin, a division of Penguin Books USA Inc. Pages 19–21, "Goodnight, Juma" from *Night on Neighborhood Street* by Eloise Greenfield. Copyright © 1991 by Eloise Greenfield. Used by permission of Dial Books for Young Readers, a division of Penguin Books USA Inc. Page 22, photograph from *Addison-Wesley Destinations in Science*. Page 27, "Sometimes" from *Fathers, Mothers, Brothers, Sisters* by Mary Ann Hoberman. Text copyright © 1991 by Mary Ann Hoberman; illustrations copyright © 1991 by Marilyn Hafner. By permission of Little, Brown and Company. Page 28–31, *Terrible, Terrible Tiger* © 1987 Colin and Jacqui Hawkins. Permission granted by the publisher Walker Books Limited. Pages 40–41, "Shopping" from *Words and Pictures* © 1991 Siobhan Dodds. Published in the UK by Walker Books Limited. Page 53, "The Farm is in a Flurry" from *Poems of A. Nonny Mouse* by Jack Prelutsky. Copyright © 1989 by Jack Prelutsky. Used by permission of Alfred A. Knopf, Inc. Pages 54–57, From *Cock-A-Doodle-Doo! What Does It Sound Like to You?* copyright © 1993 Marc Robinson and Steve Jenkins. Reprinted by permission of Stewart, Tabori & Chang, Inc. Pages 66–67, "I Spy a Butterfly" from *I Spy: A Book of Picture Riddles* by Jean Marzollo and Walter Wick. Text copyright © 1992 by Jean Marzollo; illustrations and photography copyright © 1992 by Walter Wick. Reprinted by permission of Scholastic, Inc.